MY FAVOURITE AUSSIE ANIMALS

Photography by Steve Parish

WOODLANDS

GOANNAS ARE REPTILES THAT USE

KOALAS

HEAT FROM THE SUN TO STAY WARM.

Koalas are mammals that live in trees and sleep all day.

POTOROOS

Potoroos live close to grassy woodlands where there is plenty of grass to eat.

TASMANIAN DEVILS

A Tasmanian devil's dark fur helps it hide in woodlands at night.

WOMBATS

Wombats waddle into woodlands to find roots and grasses to eat.

WEDGE-TAILED EAGLE

The wedge-tailed eagle flies over the woodlands searching for food below.

RAINFOREST

SPOTTED CUSCUS

TREE-KANGAROO

STRIPED POSSUM

Rainforest possums and tree-kangaroos are good climbers that scurry high in the treetops.

GREEN TREE PYTHON

CARPET PYTHON

PYTHON SCALES

Pythons can be very hard to see among the tree trunks and rainforest leaves.

THE SUPERB LYREBIRD

SUPERB LYREBIRD

SINGS LOVELY SONGS.

SCRATCH, SCRATCH

It scratches on the forest floor to find food and to build a "stage" to sing upon.

FRESHWATER

PLATYPUS

The strange-looking platypus swims in clear freshwater creeks and streams.

ORANGE-EYED TREE-FROGS

Male orange-eyed tree-frogs are very noisy. They gather near water to look for a mate.

SWANS AND DUCKS HAVE

BLACK SWANS

SHOVELER DUCK

WEBBED FEET FOR SWIMMING.

Black swans nibble at weeds that grow on the water or pluck plants from below the surface.

LONG-NECKED TURTLES

Long-necked turtles snap up fish, yabbies and prawns for dinner.

Frogs lay their eggs, which hatch as swimming tadpoles, in the water.

PERON'S TREE-FROG

DRY COUNTRY

DINGOES LIVE IN GROUPS

Dingoes

THAT ARE KNOWN AS PACKS.

RED KANGAROO

Dingoes attack and eat small wallabies, but red kangaroos are big enough to fight back!

KNOB-TAILED GECKO

Geckoes survive in the hot, harsh desert by hiding in cracks during the daytime.

BILBIES COME OUT AT NIGHT.

In the heat of the day, bilbies sleep in underground burrows to stay cool.

RED KANGAROOS

Red kangaroos can travel a long way to find food and to drink at a billabong.

DUCKLING

A mother duck must keep watch over her ducklings in the water while they learn to dive to search for food.

OCEAN

Many kinds of fish live in the ocean. They come in all different shapes and sizes.

Some big fish open their mouths and let small "cleanerfish" nibble off food scraps — it's just like having their teeth brushed!

CORAL TROUT & CLEANERFISH

HUMPBACK WHALES

Baby humpback whales are called "calves". Even as babies, whales are very large. Adults can even be much bigger than a bus!

DOLPHINS

BLOWHOLE

Dolphins, like whales, breathe out of a blowhole on the top of the head.

BLACKTIP REEF SHARKS

Blacktip reef sharks scan the ocean looking for schools of fish to hunt.

Clownfish make their homes inside sea anemones.

CLOWNFISH

Steve Parish is a world-famous nature photographer. His adventures with nature began when he papered his bedroom with posters and drawings of animals. Later he explored the world beneath the waves, photographing the amazing creatures there. He even discovered new species. Today he continues to make discoveries and hopes that young people will join the challenge to learn the secrets of Australia's fascinating wild creatures and their habitats.

Published by Steve Parish Publishing Pty Ltd
PO Box 1058, Archerfield, Queensland 4108 Australia

© copyright Steve Parish Publishing Pty Ltd

All rights reserved. No part of this publication may be reproduced, stored in a retrieval system, or transmitted in any form or by any means, electronic, mechanical, photocopying, recording or otherwise, without the prior permission in writing of the publisher.

ISBN 978174193651 3

First published 2010.

Photography: Steve Parish
Additional photography: p. 13 (top right), Len H. Smith
Text: Michele Perry, SPP
Design: Thomas Hamlyn-Harris, Elise Butler, SPP
Editorial: Cathy Vallance, Karin Cox & Michele Perry, SPP
Colour management: Greg Harm, SPP
Production: Jacqueline Schneider, SPP

Printed in China through Phoenix Offset

Produced in Australia at the Steve Parish Publishing Studios

www.steveparish.com.au
www.photographaustralia.com.au